Ripley's
Believe It or Not!®

Developed and produced by Ripley Publishing Ltd

This edition published and distributed by:

Mason Crest
370 Reed Road, Broomall, Pennsylvania 19008
www.masoncrest.com

Copyright © 2009 by Ripley Entertainment Inc. This edition printed in 2013. All rights reserved. Ripley's, Believe It or Not!, and Ripley's Believe It or Not! are registered trademarks of Ripley Entertainment Inc. No part of this publication may be reproduced in whole or in part, or stored in a retrieval system, or transmitted in any form or by any means, electronic, mechanical, photocopying, recording, or otherwise, without written permission from the publishers. For information regarding permission, write to VP Intellectual Property, Ripley Entertainment Inc., Suite 188, 7576 Kingspointe Parkway, Orlando, Florida, 32819
website: ripleybooks.com

Printed and bound in the United States of America.

First printing
9 8 7 6 5 4 3 2 1

Ripley's Believe It or Not!
Strange but True
ISBN-13: 978-1-4222-2573-8 (hardcover)
ISBN-13: 978-1-4222-9248-8 (e-book)
Ripley's Believe It or Not!—Complete 16 Title Series
ISBN-13: 978-1-4222-2560-8

Library of Congress Cataloging-in-Publication Data

Strange but true.
    p. cm. — (Ripley's believe it or not!)
ISBN 978-1-4222-2573-8 (hardcover) — ISBN 978-1-4222-2560-8 (series hardcover) — ISBN 978-1-4222-9248-8 (ebook)
1. Curiosities and wonders—Juvenile literature.
AG243.S398 2012
031.02—dc23
                    2012020380

PUBLISHER'S NOTE
While every effort has been made to verify the accuracy of the entries in this book, the Publisher's cannot be held responsible for any errors contained in the work. They would be glad to receive any information from readers.

WARNING
Some of the stunts and activities in this book are undertaken by experts and should not be attempted by anyone without adequate training and supervision.

![Ripley's Believe It or Not!]

Disbelief and Shock!

STRANGE BUT TRUE

www.MasonCrest.com

STRANGE BUT TRUE

Beyond belief. Be blown away by these

mind-boggling mysteries. Meet the woman who

lived with more than 5,000 scorpions for 33 days,

the man who squeezed a horse into the back

of his car, and the musician who can play

a piano while it is on fire!

Dentist Dr. Val Kolpakov has collected
nearly 1,500 different types of toothpaste
from all over the world.

Climbers Jon Ratcliffe and Steve Franklin played Scrabble while perched precariously 200 ft (60 m) above the ground on a cliff ledge in Anglesey, North Wales.

SCRABBLE FACTS

> If all the Scrabble tiles ever produced were placed in one long line, they would stretch 50,000 mi (80,500 km)—that's twice around the world.

> A giant game of Scrabble covered most of the soccer field at London's Wembley Stadium in 1998, and used letter tiles that were the size of dining tables.

> In a 1982 competition in Manchester, England, Dr. Karl Khoshnaw scored 392 points with the word "caziques"— the plural for a West Indian chief.

Even a watching alligator cannot ruffle the concentration of these two keepers at Gatorland Theme Park, Florida. "We don't set any parameters in anything that we do," said park owner Tim Williams. "We would even put the board on an alligator's back."

To celebrate the 60th anniversary of Scrabble in November 2008, extreme enthusiasts played the word game in some stunning locations—including while skydiving at an altitude of 13,000 ft (4,000 m), swimming beneath the ocean surrounded by sharks, and even just a few feet from the jaws of huge alligators!

Invented by New York architect Alfred Butts in 1948, Scrabble is produced in more than 29 languages and has sold more than 150 million sets. At least 30,000 games begin somewhere in the world every hour—but few in such crazy settings as these.

In the Lion Park, Lanseria, South Africa, gamekeepers Kevin Richard and Helga van der Merwe enjoy a game of Scrabble watched by lionesses Meg and Amy.

Using a specially reinforced wooden board and adhesive glue to make their moves, skydivers Nicole Angelides and Ramsey Kent play Scrabble at 13,000 ft (4,000 m) after throwing themselves out of a plane above Florida.

SCRABBLE

EXTREME

UPSIDE DOWN GOLDFISH

Drinkers at a pub in Devon, England, have been watching pet goldfish Aussie swim upside down for four years in a tank on the bar. The fish has become a tourist attraction, with some naturally thinking it is drunk, but experts say Aussie's unusual swimming style is down to a problem with his "swim bladder," which regulates buoyancy, and that he is as healthy as his tank companion Eddie—who swims the right way up.

Ripley's research

HOW DO FISH SWIM UPSIDE DOWN?

The ability of fish to float in water is controlled by their swim bladders, a sac filled with gas in the top part of the fish. In some fish the swim bladder can have an effect on their hearing and their sense of depth. Sometimes fish develop problems with their swim bladders, which can result in swimming to one side or even swimming upside down. From an evolutionary perspective, swim bladders are probably developed from the same air sacs that led to lungs forming in mammals.

BRACELET RETURNED ■ When Aaron Giles of Fairmont, Minnesota, lost his identity bracelet as a small boy, he never expected to see it again, but more than 25 years later it turned up—in the gizzard of a chicken. The shiny object was spotted by a meat cutter and all of the engravings were still legible.

MUMMIFIED BODY ■ A Croatian woman had sat dead in her armchair for 42 years before her mummified remains were discovered in 2008. Hedviga Golik was found in her apartment in Zagreb sitting in front of a black-and-white TV set. Neighbors had last seen her in 1966.

ARCTIC CIRCLE ■ George Porter, a British gunner, was buried in an ice floe during the 1875–76 British Arctic expedition and his body has likely been circling the North Pole for more than 130 years.

CASH DROP ■ Indonesian businessman Tung Desem Waringin dropped $10,700 in banknotes from a plane in 2008 to promote his new motivational book and help the country's poor people. His plane circled eight times over a sports field in the town of Serang, scattering bills to the crowds who had gathered below.

NAME CHANGE ■ Chicago school bus driver Steve Kreuscher filed a petition to change his name to "In God We Trust" because he was worried that the phrase might be removed from U.S. currency.

BANK ERROR ■ In 2007, a New York bank accidentally gave $2 million of a client's money to another customer with the same name. Benjamin Lovell tried to explain to the bank attendant that he did not have a $5-million account, but the bank insisted it was his money and that he was able to withdraw it, so he did. He was later brought before a court on a charge of grand larceny.

UNIDENTIFIED FLYING OBJECT ■ A hook-shaped piece of metal, 16 in (40 cm) in length, fell from the sky in October 2007 and crashed through the roof of an unoccupied car in Stanton, Delaware. The mysterious object was too hot to handle after its descent and left ash on the driver's seat. The Federal Aviation Authority said it had definitely not fallen from an airplane.

Gum Sucker

Despite the increased use of Western medicine, blood-sucking leeches are still a popular medical procedure in India. Applied to the gums, or elsewhere on the body, they are thought to cure a variety of ailments, including blood and immunity disorders.

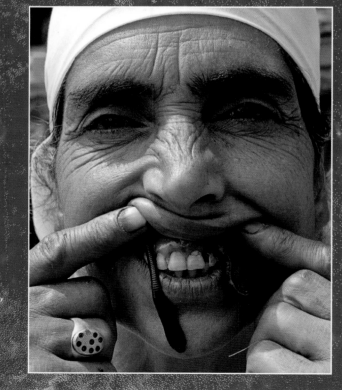

BATHROOM GIFTS ■ In the summer of 2007, an anonymous man left more than 400 envelopes in bathrooms of public buildings all across Japan, each containing a letter and cash worth $85.

LEG THIEVES ■ Thinking it was a source of holy healing powers, thieves in Tirupati, Andhra Pradesh, India, sawed the leg off an 80-year-old holy man and stole it. They plied their victim with alcohol and removed his leg when he had passed out drunk. Despite heavy loss of blood, the holy man survived his ordeal.

FISHY FIND ■ On January 24, 2008, ship captain Kiyoshi Kimino found a 15-year-old handwritten letter from a schoolchild, which read, "I'm a first-grade student. Our school is 120 years old. We are now celebrating it. If you happen to find this letter, please write back to me." Even more unusual, the letter was found stuck to the back of a flatfish off the coast of Japan.

HAIR CUT ■ Scissor-wielding bandits aboard a bus in Rio de Janeiro, Brazil, grabbed a 22-year-old woman's hair, twisted it into a ponytail and cut it off. Police think the thieves were hoping to sell the long black hair, which the woman had been growing for four years, to wig-makers or to hair-transplant centers.

FORGETFUL THIEF ■ A shoplifter seeking to make a quick getaway from a Dutch supermarket after stealing a packet of meat left behind a crucial piece of evidence—his 12-year-old son. The thief was in such a hurry that he forgot all about the boy, who quickly furnished the police with his father's details.

SECRET TUNNEL ■ A man wanted for the murder of a neighbor hid for 17 years in a tunnel he dug under his home. Hui Guangwen was eventually discovered at the house in Suinan, China, in 2007, following a tip-off to police. He told them: "It was really boring down there."

STUD STUNNER ■ Three days after losing a nose stud in a fall while kneeboarding from a speedboat off Tasmania, Kirsty Brittain was standing next to her fiancé when he filleted a fish he had just caught—and inside the fish was the missing stud.

SNAKE MAN ■ A 19-year-old Kosovan prisoner, who weighed less than 121 lb (55 kg), escaped from a jail cell in Linz, Austria, in 2008 by squeezing through a narrow food hatch in the cell door.

MISSING TEETH ■ After Qin Yuan from Chongqing, China, woke up missing his dentures and with a strange feeling in his body, he consulted doctors who discovered his false teeth lodged in one of his lungs. After operating, they suggested that he take them out before sleeping.

EGG SURPRISE ■ When Mr. Cao from Changchun, China, cracked open an egg to make his supper, he was shocked to find a live chick inside—and he was even more surprised to find that the chick had four legs!

ROOF REPAIRS ■ A man who was trying to repair the roof of his home in Beijing, China, was blown up a nearby tree by a sudden gust of wind. He was left clinging to the 45-ft-high (14-m) tree for 20 minutes until firefighters rescued him.

ANCIENT STRING ■ Unearthing a Stone Age settlement on the Isle of Wight, England, archeologists found an 8,000-year-old piece of string. It was made from twisted plant stems.

COFFIN HOME ■ Despite having a morbid fear of being buried alive, a Brazilian man has set up house in a large coffin. Freud de Melo has equipped the coffin with a TV, a water pitcher, an air vent, and two plastic tubes that he attaches to megaphones to contact the outside world.

UNINVITED GUEST ■ Over Christmas 2008, a stranger spent several days secretly living in the roof of a family's house in Wilkes-Barre, Pennsylvania. The Ferrance family discovered the uninvited guest only when he emerged from their attic wearing their clothes. He had been staying with neighbors but, when they told him to leave, he went through a trap door into the shared attic.

SLEEP SURFER ■ A woman turned on her computer, typed in her username and password, then composed and sent three emails—all while she was asleep. Researchers from the University of Toledo, Ohio, said the sleepwalker learned what she had done when someone contacted her about one of her emails the following day.

WRAPPED UP

Now in her late eighties, Zhou Guizhen from Liuyi, China, had her feet bound when she was young, in an ancient Chinese custom. Girls would have their toes broken and tied underneath their feet before the arch of the foot could develop, so that the toes never grew properly and the feet could fit in tiny shoes.

HORSE WON'T FIAT

When a Polish farmer bought a foal at auction in Warsaw in January 2009, the only way to get it back to his farm, 150 mi (241 km) away, was to put it in the back of a small hatchback with the rear seats strapped to the roof! Luckily, the police found the car on the highway after it had broken down, and took custody of the 260-lb (117-kg) horse until they could find a better means of transport.

FATAL FLAW ■ A man who copied an episode of *CSI: Crime Scene Investigation* by committing suicide but trying to make it look like murder was found out because he didn't attach enough helium balloons to the gun with which he had shot himself. Planning for the gun to float away, Thomas Hickman drove from Dallas, Texas, into New Mexico and put duct tape over his mouth before shooting himself in the head. However, the bundle of balloons, with the gun still attached, was found snagged on bushes nearby.

FLORAL APOLOGY ■ A prisoner who escaped from jail in Crawford County, Arkansas, in June 2008, left behind an origami flower—made from toilet paper—as his way of saying sorry for breaking free.

GROUP TRANCE ■ Fifty female workers at a garment factory in Tangerang, Indonesia, went into an involuntary collective trance in 2007, during which they wept uncontrollably and jerked their bodies around.

RADIOACTIVE CAFÉ ■ Police in the Ukraine foiled a plot to smuggle a highly radioactive helicopter from the site of the Chernobyl disaster area and turn it into a unique coffee shop. Several people were detained in May 2008 while transporting the scrap helicopter—which seated up to 28 people but emitted 30 times the legal level of radiation—from within the exclusion zone set up around the Chernobyl nuclear power station that exploded in 1986.

Dog Girl

Oxana Malaya acts like a dog, walking on all fours, panting with her tongue hanging out and whining and barking at will. Her canine behavior is a legacy of her feral childhood. For five years from the age of three, she was raised by a pack of wild dogs near the village of Novaya Blagoveschenka, Ukraine, after apparently being abandoned by her parents. When she was finally discovered in 1991, she had almost forgotten how to speak.

UNLUCKY CAR ■ Hollywood star James Dean died at age 24 in 1955 when he crashed his Porsche Spyder sports car. The car was taken to a garage, where the engine slipped out and fell onto a mechanic, shattering both of his legs. The engine was then bought by a doctor who put it in his racing car and was soon killed in a crash. Another driver in that same race was killed in his car, which had Dean's driveshaft fitted to it. When the shell of Dean's Porsche was later repaired and put on display, the showroom burned down. Exhibited again in Sacramento, it fell off the stand on to a visitor, breaking his hip. Finally, in 1959, the car mysteriously broke into 11 pieces while sitting on steel supports.

NAME GAME ■ Three Englishmen, traveling separately through Peru in the 1920s, found themselves the only passengers in a railroad car. Introducing themselves to each other, they discovered that one man's surname was Bingham, the second man's was Powell, and the third man's was Bingham-Powell. None of the men were related to either of the others in any way.

SICK ROBBER ■ An Australian post office thief was caught by his own vomit. Ahmed Habib Jalloul was so nervous during the robbery in Adelaide that he was physically sick on the spot, allowing police to take DNA from the pool of vomit and match it to him.

PRISON WORSHIP ■ In December 2007, inmate Michael Polk sued Utah prison officials because they wouldn't provide a Thor's hammer, a prayer cloth, a wassail-filled horn, a boar-skin drum, and a sword—so that he could worship the ancient Norse gods.

FAKE WIFE ■ When an Indian man went to court in 2008 to obtain a divorce, he took along an impersonator in place of his wife. The supposedly mutual divorce was granted immediately, but when his real wife found out and appealed, the divorce was suspended.

DEAD MAN ELECTED ■ Neculai Ivascu was re-elected as mayor for the village of Voinesti, Romania, in June 2008—despite being dead. He died from liver disease shortly after voting began but still beat his living opponent, Gheorghe Dobrescu, by 23 votes.

GRUESOME DELIVERY ■ Two sisters living a mile and a half apart in Greenville, South Carolina, had bags containing human body parts left outside their homes on the same morning in April 2008. Each bag contained a human hand and a human foot.

LOST BALL ■ When a conifer was felled at the Eaton Golf Club in Norwich, Norfolk, England, in February 2009, the greenkeeper was amazed to discover a perfectly preserved golf ball embedded deep in the trunk. The tree had apparently grown around the ball, which is believed to have lodged in a fork of the tree many years ago following a wayward drive at the first hole.

CORPSE RIDE ■ Two men wheeled their dead friend through the streets of New York City in an office chair in January 2008 to cash his $355 Social Security check. All charges against them were later dropped because they said they didn't know he was dead at the time.

GRISLY DISCOVERY ■ The corpse of Vladimir Ledenev of Tula, Russia, was found sitting at his kitchen table in January 2007—where it had sat undisturbed for six years. In front of him were an empty vodka bottle and a glass.

LONG WAIT ■ Schoolgirl Emily Hwaung of Seattle, Washington, put a note into an ocean-bound soda bottle and received a reply from 1,735 mi (2,790 km) away—21 years later. The bottle, with its message still intact, was washed ashore in Nelson Lagoon, Alaska, and picked up by Merle Brandell, who managed to trace Emily via her old school.

RING RETRIEVED ■ A grandmother from Leicestershire, England, was reunited with her engagement ring—67 years after she had thrown it into a field during an argument. Violet Booth and her fiancé hunted in vain for the ring and had to buy another when they got married a few months later in 1941, but in 2008 her grandson, metal-detector fan Leighton Boyes, amazingly dug up the ring after pinpointing the spot where it had landed.

ROMEO ROBBER ■ An Italian thief who fell in love with the female cashier at a Genoa post office he robbed was arrested when he went back to ask her for a date. The day after forcing the 21-year-old to hand over money at gunpoint, the robber returned to the scene of the crime with a bunch of flowers, an apology, and the offer of a date. Instead of immediately accepting his offer, the cashier kept him talking while she activated a silent alarm connected to the police station.

MOVIE MEMENTO ■ Workmen draining a lake beneath a roller coaster in Blackpool, England, in 2005, discovered an earring that had been lost by Hollywood movie star Marlene Dietrich 73 years earlier. The precious pearl earring had fallen off while Dietrich was taking a ride on the Big Dipper at the resort's Pleasure Beach in 1934.

Roadquill

Canadian artist Amy Nugent trawls the streets looking for roadkill, then collects it as material for incredible artwork. She hoarded more than 30,000 porcupine quills from Canadian roads to make a large sphere that she calls Roadquill. Her work is dedicated to recycling and honoring the animals that she encounters.

Ripley's
Believe It or Not!

MUSICAL FLAME

Japanese jazz pianist Yosuke Yamashita wore a flame-retardant suit while playing an improvised piece for ten minutes on a piano on fire—until the blaze snapped the strings.

Star Wars Wedding

When Star Wars *fans Rebecca D'Madeiros and Bill Duda were married in their Portland, Oregon, backyard in June 2008, they insisted that all 70 guests come as characters from the 1970s sci-fi movie. The bride and groom were dressed as Mon Mothma and Admiral Ackbar respectively, the wedding was presided over by Yoda, who had recently secured his marriage license over the Internet, and the ringbearer was Princess Leia. The happy couple were led from the house by a line of Imperial Stormtroopers.*

DELAYED DELIVERY ■ Michael Cioffi of Boston, Massachusetts, received a postcard of Yellowstone National Park's Tower Falls in February 2008—79 years after it was sent.

FUNERAL FAN Mijo Tkalcec from Peteranec, Croatia, has been to over 2,000 funerals. He has been fascinated by them since he was a child and will travel hundreds of miles just to attend one.

SAME BIRTHDAYS ■ Martin and Kim MacKriell from Gloucester, England, are unlikely ever to forget their three children's birthdays, because they were all born on January 29—at odds of 133,000 to one. Their son Robin was born on January 29, 1994, daughter Rebecca was born on January 29, 1996, and although another daughter Ruby was due to be born on February 7, 2008, she had to be delivered by cesarean section and the only available date was the same birthday as her siblings.

PHOTOGRAPHIC MEMORY ■ Karen and Mark Cline of Mansfield, Ohio, did not have $150 to pay a photographer for their wedding photos when they got married as teenagers in 1980. But when photographer Jim Wagner discovered the pictures during a clearout, he remembered the impoverished couple and sent them their wedding photos just in time for their 27th anniversary.

SPENDING SPREE ■ A nine-year-old Indonesian boy went on a five-day spending spree in 2008 that cost his parents $10,000. Ahmad Legal Civiandi spent his family's cash savings on toys and gadgets.

DOUBLE DEATH ■ After 70 years of marriage, a Syrian couple died of natural causes on the same day in January 2008. The 95-year-old husband died hours after his 90-year-old wife passed away.

JEDI ATTACK ■ A *Star Wars* fan who cofounded the Church of the Jedi in Wales was assaulted in 2008 by a man dressed as Darth Vader. Barney Jones—a.k.a. Master Jonba Hehol—was hit on the head with a metal crutch by Darth Vader impersonator Arwel Hughes.

SECRET GUEST ■ A homeless woman managed to live undetected in the closet of a man's house for a whole year. She sneaked into the house in Kasuya, Japan, when he left it unlocked and set up home in the top compartment of his closet without him having any idea of her presence. She moved a mattress into the small shelf space, took showers while he was out, and left no trace of her existence. It was only when food mysteriously began disappearing from his kitchen that he became suspicious and police found the 58-year-old woman curled up on the closet shelf.

SURPRISE DISCOVERY ■ Steve Flaig of Plainfield Township, Michigan, had searched for his birth mother for a long time and in December 2007 he finally tracked her down—finding to his amazement that they had been working for the same company for almost a year. He was a delivery driver for a local home-improvement store and his mother was the woman he simply knew as Chris, the head cashier.

ANONYMOUS DONOR ■ Every month for 33 years, an anonymous donor has left a money-filled envelope at a police station in Tochigi, Japan, with instructions to help the needy.

NO DEATHS ■ In 1946, Mildred West, an obituary writer on New York's *Alton Evening Telegraph*, took a week's vacation. During her absence and for the first time in the newspaper's history, there were no deaths in Alton (population 32,000). Normally, they averaged ten a week.

SKIPPING SCHOOL ■ Ten-year-old Diego Palacios of Monterrey, Mexico, used industrial glue to affix his hand to his bed's metal frame—to avoid going to school.

SINISTER KIMONO ■ A kimono owned successively by three teenage girls, each of whom had died before having a chance to wear it, was considered so unlucky that it was cremated by a priest in 1657. But as the garment burned, a wind fanned the flames and started a fire that destroyed three-quarters of Tokyo, demolishing 9,000 shops, 500 palaces, 300 temples, and 61 bridges, and killing 100,000 people.

SNAIL MAIL ■ A postcard from Nebraska mailed on December 23, 1914, finally reached Oberlin, Kansas, in 2007—93 years late!

DOUBLE RESCUE ■ A Chinese man, Wang Weiqing, rescued a seven-year-old boy from a pond in Beicheng in 2008—20 years after rescuing the boy's father from exactly the same spot.

RESTRAINED DRIVER ■ A burglary suspect embarrassed police in Brisbane, Australia, in April 2008 by driving off in their patrol car—even though he had handcuffs on. While the arresting officers were searching for further evidence, the handcuffed man climbed into the driver's seat, started the engine and drove off.

SIBLING RIVALRY ■ The mayor of an Ohio village fought off a challenge for power in November 2007—from her younger brother. Daniel Huffman was hoping to unseat his sister, Charlotte Garman, in the election, but the registered voters of Montezuma stayed loyal to Garman, who had been mayor for eight years, by 43 votes to 24.

CUTLERY ESCAPE ■ In May 2008, 36 prisoners escaped from a jail in N'Zerekore, Guinea, by using spoons to dig through a wall.

WALLET RECOVERED ■ Tom Eichenberg of Elk Grove, California, had his wallet returned to him in 2008—33 years after he lost it. He mislaid the wallet while he was a student at Santa Clara University in 1975 and it was eventually found nestled in a wall by construction workers renovating the student center.

TOILET CORPSE ■ A family lived for two months in 2008 with the decaying body of a 90-year-old woman on the toilet of the only bathroom in their home in Necedah, Wisconsin. They were said to be following the advice of a religious leader who told them the corpse would come back to life.

MACHINERY SPLIT ■ A Serb farmer, angry at a court order forcing him to share everything with his ex-wife, took the judge at his word and cut all his farm tools and machinery in half using a grinder.

Oh baby!

When her daughter said she wanted a sibling, Deborah King made her one—from vinyl. Deborah from Edinburgh, Scotland, is an expert in "reborning," a hobby that creates amazingly lifelike baby dolls. The dolls are painted with multiple layers to give a mottled-skin effect and are weighted and stuffed to weigh and feel similar to a real baby. Customers, who include grieving parents and nostalgic grandparents, can even ask for a heartbeat to be added to their reborn baby.

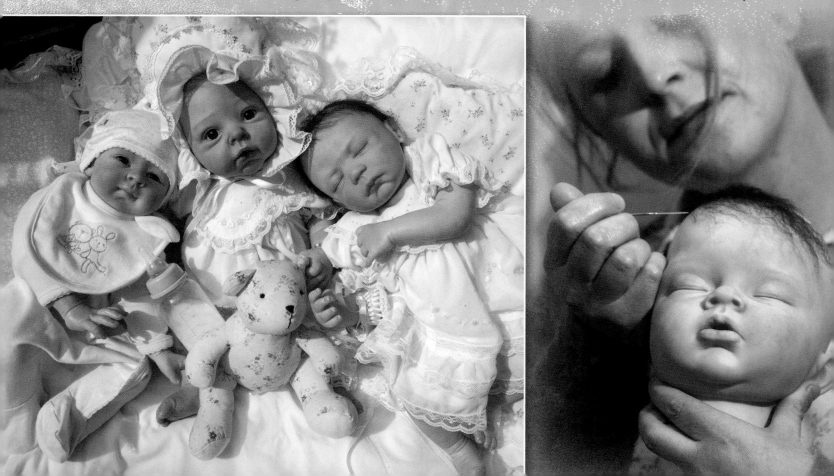

BARNUM AND BAILEY
GREATEST SHOW ON EARTH

Wowing circus audiences across the U.S.A. for more than 20 years, the Ringling Brothers and Barnum and Bailey Circus sideshow was a result of a merger between two of the largest circuses in the world, which were combined in 1919 to make the "Greatest Show on Earth." The circus traveled in 100 double-length railroad cars and employed more than 1,200 people—it was probably the largest traveling circus that there had ever been. It followed that the new, combined sideshow was one of the biggest of its kind and the show's *spieler*, or "talker," boasted that they had "more freaks, wonders, strange and unusual people than any other traveling museum, circus, or sideshow in the entire world."

At one point, there were more than 30 oddities on show. Audiences would pay to see the acts before the main event opened in the big tent and could buy merchandise from the performers, such as rings belonging to giants and authentic stories of their unusual lives. Such opportunities meant that popular acts often became very wealthy.

The Bearded Girl

Annie Jones began working on the Barnum stage at only nine months old and stayed for most of her life, becoming a spokesperson for the circus.

Dog Face

"Jojo the Dog Face Boy" was the Russian Fedor Jefticheive who performed with his hairy father at sideshows from the late 19th century and later became a popular act in his own right with the P.T. Barnum Circus. Jojo would play up to his wolf boy character by growling at the crowd, although he was intelligent and could speak five languages. He died of pneumonia in 1905 in Greece.

Anna Haining Bates

The circus performer Anna Haining Bates was born in Canada in 1846 and had grown to over 7 ft 6 in (2.3 m) in height when she was hired by the P.T. Barnum Circus in 1862. It was there that she met and married the 8-ft-tall (2.4-m) Captain Martin Van Buren Bates.

Clico

Clico's real name was Franz Taaibosh. He was a South African dancer brought to sideshow fame by a Westerner, Captain Heston. He was so called because of the "clicking" sounds of his native language, and performed with the Ringling Circus for many years.

CLICO Wild Dancing

SOUTH AFRICAN BUSHMAN

Barnum's Freaks

The "museum" was part of P.T. Barnum's traveling circus: from left to right are featured Laloo, who had two bodies, Young Herman with a hugely expanding chest, J.K. Coffey with the body of a skeleton, James Morris, who could stretch his skin to extremes, and Jojo the Dog Face Boy.

oll amily idgets

CELEBRATING "RING
RINGLING BROTHERS AND BARNUM

-1933-

"GOLDEN JUBILEE"

EY COMBINED CIRCUS SIDE SHOW

PHOTO BY
E.J.KELTY
CENTURY
74 W 47 ST.

1 → 25 See pages 20–21 for who everybody is

① ELSA VAN DORYSON
7 ft 8 in (2.3 m)—Giant

Born in Berlin, Germany, in 1888, Elsa Van Doryson (real name Dora Herms) was shorter than her theatrical "sister" but still towered over audiences at 7 ft 8 in (2.3 m) tall. She was so tall while still in her teens that she appeared in a German show demonstrating extremes of the body. She joined the Barnum and Bailey Circus in 1914, and toured Europe with her giant husband Werner Syre until she became a fixture in the sideshow from 1922.

② ALFRED LANGEVIN
Smoked Through His Eyes

Alfred Langevin was a regular Ripley's oddity, performing his strange optical act for audiences at the Odditorium from 1933 to 1940. Experts believe that an abnormality in his tear glands allowed Alfred to blow up balloons, play the recorder and even smoke a cigarette by forcing air out of his eyes.

③ ⑥ ⑲ & ㉑ HARRY DOLL
The Doll Family of Midgets

Harry Doll was the head of a "family of dolls" that toured with the Ringling Brothers and Barnum and Bailey sideshow. They were real siblings born to a couple from Stolpen, Germany. Harry and Gracie began in German sideshows where they were spotted by the American Bert W. Earles, who took them to live with him in California and enrolled them in the 101 Ranch Wild West Show in 1914. Some years later they were joined by Daisy and Tiny and became a part of the Ringling Brothers and Barnum and Bailey Circus where they entertained audiences for 30 years. Eventually named the "dolls" after members of the audience described them as such, they would ride horses and sing and dance in the sideshow. The family branched out into Hollywood when all four appeared as munchkins in the 1939 film The Wizard of Oz, and Harry and Gracie played significant parts in the 1932 horror movie Freaks. One of the longest running sideshow acts in the U.S.A., Harry was born in 1902 and died aged 83, Gracie was born in 1899 and died aged 71, Daisy was born in 1907 and died aged 72, while Tiny was born in 1914 and died in 2004 aged 90.

④ VITO BASSILE
The Vegetable King

⑤ MOSSAB HABIB
Egyptian Wonder Worker

⑥ GRACIE DOLL
(see Harry Doll, left)

⑦ MAJOR MITE
26 in (0.67 m) and 20 lb (9 kg)

As well as being a successful draw on the sideshow circuit, Major Mite was one of the smallest munchkins in The Wizard of Oz film and played a number of other parts in Hollywood films, including the role of a thief disguised as a baby in Free Eats (1932). He died in 1975, aged 62, in Salem where he was born and originally named Clarence Chesterfield Howerton.

⑧ JACK EARLE
Claimed to be 8 ft 6 in (2.6 m) tall

Joining the Barnum and Bailey Circus in the mid-1920s, Jack Earle was claimed to be an enormous 8 ft 6 in (2.6 m). Such was his imposing stature that he was recruited to play the role of the giant in the 1924 film Jack and the Beanstalk. After he stopped performing in the Ringling sideshow, Jack became a salesman and a successful photographer and poet.

⑨ LIA GRAFF
Smallest Woman on Earth

⑩ BARON PAUCCI
24 in (0.6 m)

Baron Paucci had a loud demeanor that belied his tiny stature and earned him a reputation as a gambler and big spender. He performed at Sam Gumpertz's show on Coney Island for 15 years, joining many other midgets in a scaled-down town called Lilliputia named after the place in the book Gulliver's Travels. When his outrageous behavior forced him to leave Coney Island, he found a place in the Ringling Circus sideshow. Baron Paucci married a woman of normal size, but the marriage was short-lived.

⑪ JACK HUBER
Armless Man

⑫ SUZANNE
Snake Trainer

Suzanne was billed as "the greatest of all the snake trainers!" She is seen here with a baby boa constrictor around her neck but also used to show larger snakes up to 20 ft (6 m) in length.

⑬ MISS MAE
Tattooed Girl

⑭ CLICO
The Wild Dancing South African Bushman

A skilled dancer, South African tribesman Franz Taaibosh was referred to as Clico because of the clicks he used in his own language on stage. He was discovered by a Captain Heston, who promoted Clico's shows in Europe before the outbreak of World War I. Clico impressed Americans who were watching and he joined Sam Gumpertz's Coney Island show before touring with the Ringling Brothers for many years. He died aged 83 in 1940 in New York.

⑮ HILDA VAN DORYSON
8 ft 4 in (2.5 m)

The stage sister of Elsa Van Doryson, Hilda was born Annie Haase in 1906 in Europe. When her early showbusiness career fell flat after a staged marriage to another giant, she joined Elsie in 1926 for the first time as "sisters." They played sideshows together until 1939, and Annie Haase was performing in the late-1960s under her old stage name Kaatje Van Dyk. She was recognized in 1968 as the tallest woman in the world.

⑯ DAN BREWER
Inside Lecturer

The show also featured a lecturer, who explained to the amazed audience the extraordinary sights before their eyes.

⑰ FRANCISCO LENTINI
Three-legged Man

One of 12 children, Francisco Lentini was born in Rosolini, Italy, in 1889. He had his malformed twin brother's leg attached to his side, and a small foot-like growth on his third leg, technically giving him four feet, each of different lengths, and 16 toes. Despite his disability, Francisco approached life with a passion and after seeing children at a disabled school in a worse predicament than himself, the young Lentini learned to ride a bike and skate on ice. He arrived in America when only eight years old, but became an overnight sensation, popular for his stage humor, kicking a soccer ball with his extra leg and sitting on it like a bar stool. He performed at Coney Island and with the Ringling Brothers and Barnum and Bailey sideshows for more than 40 years until he died in 1966 aged 78.

⑱ THELMA AND DORIS PATTON
Albino Twins of unknown origin

⑲ TINY DOLL
(see Harry Doll, opposite)

⑳ DAINTY DOLLY
555 lb (250 kg) at 4 ft 11 in (1.5 m)

Dainty Dolly's name suited her as a normal healthy baby in Cincinnati in 1901, but she began to grow fast. Aged 26, she was found by a traveling carnival owner to be a lot heavier than his own Fat Lady and was quickly offered a job in his show. Under his guidance, 500-lb (227-kg) Celesta Herrmann soon became Dainty Dolly and under a strict diet regime of 10,000 calories a day—almost five times the recommended amount—she ballooned to more than 555 lb (250 kg) and, at only 4 ft 11 in (1.5 m) tall, required 36 ft (11 m) of cloth for her stage costume. Dainty Dolly suffered a heart attack as she neared 50 years old, but responded by losing an incredible 443 lb (201 kg) in just over a year by eating only baby food.

㉑ DAISY DOLL
(see Harry Doll, opposite)

㉒ EKO AND IKO
Albino Twins

The black albino twins Eko and Iko boast one of the most remarkable stories in circus sideshow history. It started dramatically in 1899 when they were kidnapped by sideshow bounty hunters for their unique appearance. They were variously known as "Ecuadorian Cannibals," "The Sheep-Headed Men" and the "Ambassadors from Mars." They were not paid for their early performances with the Barnes circus. Later they started to tour with the Ringling Brothers and Barnum and Bailey sideshow, where, in 1927, their mother rediscovered them and demanded that they be freed from performing or she would sue. They were freed, but returned to the sideshow in 1928 with a contract that ensured them a great deal of money as they played venues like Madison Square Garden to more than 10,000 people. They toured the world in the 1930s, performing for the Queen of England among others, and returned to the U.S.A. to perform right up until 1961.

㉓ ZIP AND IZIT
Ituri Pygmies ("Pinheads")

The "pinhead" was an enduring feature of circus sideshows—it usually referred to people born with a condition known as microcephaly, which resulted in an unusually small head. The most famous "pinhead" was William Henry Johnson, born in New Jersey but transformed by P.T. Barnum into a wild-man character supposedly found during a hunting trip in Africa. Although William was an American, he would howl and rattle the bars of a cage for his act. Over the years, he was known as "The Monkey Man," "The Missing Link," the "What is it?" and "Zip, the Pinhead."

㉔ MARTIN LAURELLO
The Human Owl

Born Martin Emmerling in the 1890s, Martin "The Human Owl" Laurello could perform a painful-looking rotation of the head to 180 degrees, at Coney Island and Ringling Brothers. Later in his career, he was swiveling his head at the Ripley's Believe It or Not! Odditorium. After taking his act around Europe, he made it across the Atlantic in 1921, along with several other European "freaks" hired to perform at the Coney Island Dreamland.

㉕ P.J. STAUNTON
Assistant Manager

㉖ JEANIE TOMAINI
The Half Girl

Born without legs in 1916 in Indiana, Jeanie was just 2 ft 6 in (76 cm) tall as an adult. When she was still a child her family was approached by a local fair—a meeting that resulted in Jeanie appearing at fairs and circuses across the country. She met her future husband Aurelio "Al" Tomaini, a giant who stood more than 8 ft (2.4 m) tall, while working on sideshows. Jeanie and Al retired in the 1940s to live in Florida, where Jeanie passed away in 1999, aged 82 years.

Turn over to see more

ALL IN THE THREE RINGS AT ONE TIME

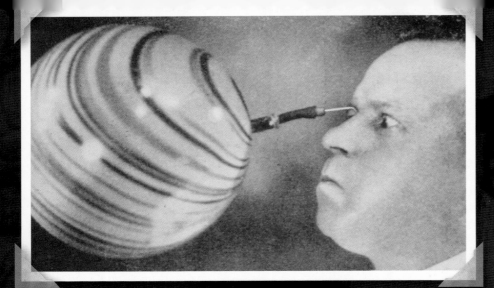

Alfred Langevin

Alfred Langevin could blow up balloons, smoke cigarettes, and even blow out candles by forcing air out of his eyes. He was a regular at the Ripley's Odditorium.

Eko and Iko

Albino twins, Eko and Iko were kidnapped by bounty hunters working for sideshow talent scouts in the late 19th century, but were later freed and became wealthy performers for the Ringling Brothers and Barnum and Bailey Circus sideshow.

MAJOR MITE
AGE -- 18 YEARS
WEIGHT - 19 POUNDS
HEIGHT - 26 INCHES

Major Mite

Major Mite performed at the Ringling Brothers and Barnum and Bailey Circus sideshow and was one of the munchkins in the 1939 film The Wizard of Oz.

Hairy Family

Known as "The Sacred Hairy Family from Burma," two family members had faces completely covered in thick hair. After performing for the King of Burma, they were discovered by an Englishman and were one of the attractions at the P.T. Barnum Circus in the 1890s.

DEAD CAT ■ Edwin Julius Krueger, who ran a general store in Wykoff, Minnesota, for over 50 years, never threw anything away. Following his death in 1989, the store became a museum, full of Krueger's accumulated artifacts including decades of junk mail, 35 years' worth of TV guides, his collection of *Smokey the Bear* posters, and even his dead cat Sammy, who died in 1986 and is kept on a shelf in a small cardboard box.

HIP JOINT ■ Prague lawyer Premsyl Donat tried to sell what he claimed was the Czech president's hip joint on eBay in August 2008. Bidding had reached $40,000 when the police swooped in and revealed that the joint was not, in fact, that of President Vaclav Klaus who had undergone a hip replacement operation three months earlier.

CLOSE RELATIVES ■ Lewis Manilow, 81, and Jack Shore, 82, of Chicago, Illinois, who lived only six blocks apart, met randomly in 2008 and then discovered that they were brothers.

ESCAPE BID ■ A daring escape bid through the air-conditioning ducts of the Alton city jail, Texas, in 2008, ended abruptly when one of the two prisoners crashed through the ceiling into the office of Police Chief Baldemar Flores.

HIDING PLACE ■ After spending four years on the run from police on suspicion of robbery, Petru Susanu was finally found in 2009—hiding under his mother's bed. He had used floorboards and carpet to construct a makeshift hideaway under the double bed at the family home in Vladeni, Romania.

License Plate Omen

In an incredible coincidence, Dominic Calgi of New Rochelle, New York, owned a car with the license plate 5V 17 32, which spelled out the exact date of his death—May 17, 1932.

UNTIMELY PROPHECY ■ A bag snatcher in Venice, Italy, died from a heart attack in 2008, minutes after his 66-year-old victim had yelled at him: "I hope you drop dead!"

JUNK PILE ■ Police carted away more than two tons of garbage from the home of Hiroshi Sekine of Gyoda, Siatama, Japan, after he was arrested for blocking the sidewalk with junk.

EDIBLE ORGANS

It looks like a prop from an old horror movie, but it's actually a tasty cake painstakingly made to look like a bloody chest cavity. The "Thorax Cake" was created by horror enthusiast Barbara Jo from San José, California. Different flavor cakes were filled with raspberry, strawberry, kiwi, mango, and blueberry sauces designed to ooze out of the organs when sliced into. The gruesome creation was held together by a white-chocolate rib cage before being devoured at Barbara's annual pumpkin-carving party.

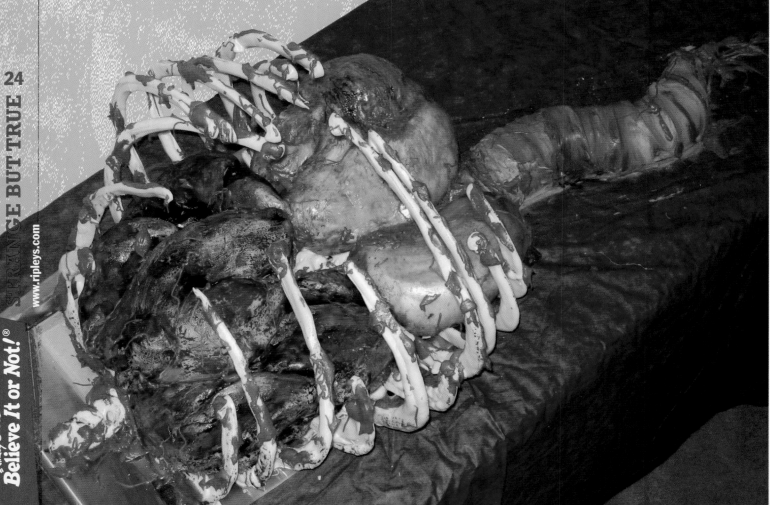

HAIR-RAISING RIDE ■ Fifth-grader Mason Calderhead from Mooresville, Indiana, was surprised to hear a familiar meow when he got out of his mom's car after traveling from his home to karate class in February 2009. His pet cat Gurdy had somehow attached herself to the underside of the car and had taken a hair-raising 5-mi (8-km) ride. Luckily, Gurdy suffered no injuries, but was just a little shaken up from her experience.

KLINGON KEYBOARD ■ A keyboard featuring letters from *Star Trek's* Klingon alphabet has been marketed in Britain. It has been designed for science-fiction fans who have learned the alien tongue Klingonese, the most widely spoken fictional language in the world. The Bible and the works of Shakespeare have already been translated into Klingonese.

LATE VERDICT ■ Although her son had been deceased for two years, Julie Strange of Cumbria, England, carried his ashes into a courtroom so he could answer a summons charge that the judge refused to drop.

BUN FIGHT ■ After arguing with his girlfriend in 2008, a 22-year-old man from Vero Beach, Florida, was charged with assaulting her—having shoved a cheeseburger in her face.

BARBER LAW ■ It's against the law in Houma, Louisiana, to operate barber shops on Sundays and Mondays. Just ask barber Clyde Scott, who was caught working on Monday, May 19, 2008—and ticketed.

EMU CRASH ■ A woman from Largs Bay, South Australia, was killed in January 2008 when her motorbike crashed into an emu that was running across the highway in broad daylight.

KEEN COP ■ Having been in the police force for only six days, P.C. John Nash of Greater Manchester Police, England, was so keen to make his first arrest that he chased, and apprehended, a suspect despite having a 6-in (15-cm) twig impaled in his left eye.

CHEAP HIT ■ Oofty Goofty, a 19th-century sideshow performer in San Francisco, California, carried a baseball bat with him and offered to let people hit him with it for 50 cents a swing.

TATTOO CLUE ■ Arrested in St. Paul, Minnesota, in December 2008, a 25-year-old driver tried to get away with his crime by giving a false name to the arresting police officers—forgetting that his real name was tattooed in large letters on his neck.

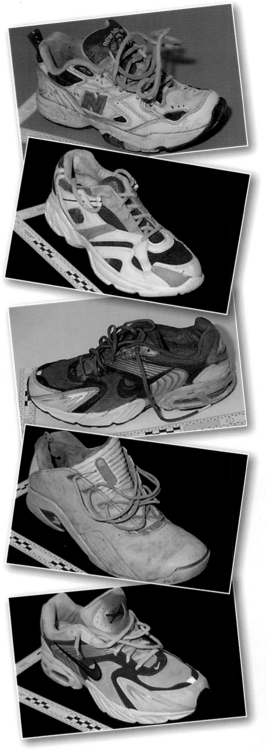

Pigeon Impact

Pigeons can fly at 50 mph (80 km/h), so when a pigeon flew at full tilt into a second-floor window in Washington, D.C., in October 2008, it left an almost perfect impression on the glass, including wings, beak, and tail.

Washed-up Feet

Police were mystified by the grisly discovery of five feet washed up in different locations in Canada between August 2007 and June 2008. Each of the sneakers had human feet still inside, which eventually enabled a coroner to identify two pairs, belonging to two unidentified persons. The fifth shoe remained a mystery. It is estimated that a foot separated from a drowned body could travel by strong currents around 1,000 mi (1,600 km) before reaching land.

Ripley's—
Believe It or Not!®

Sting in the Tail

In previous *Ripley's Believe It or Not!* annuals, we saw Thailand's "Scorpion Queen" Kanchana Kaetkaew get married with live scorpions on her dress and survive 32 days locked up with more than 3,000 scorpions. Now she has shocked people further by living in a room for 33 days with 5,000 large scorpions for company from December 2008 to January 2009. The creepy-crawly lover was stung three times in her room at the *Ripley's Believe It or Not!* museum in Pattaya, Thailand, but luckily she has built up immunity to the venom over the years and was unharmed.

℞ Ripley's research

Scorpions are generally timid, but they will defend themselves with the very painful sting on their tail, and some species can produce enough venom to kill a human. In the U.S.A. there are about 1,000 scorpion stings reported each year, although the last known death was in 1968. In Mexico, however, there are more than 1,000 deaths from scorpion stings every year.

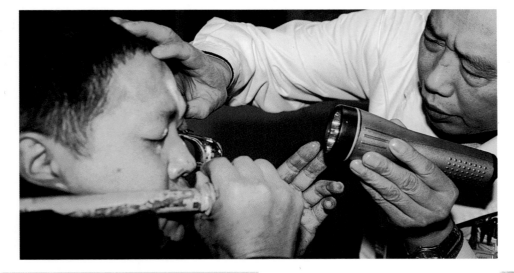

Eye Watering

When Yi Zhao of Chongqing, China, slipped in the bath at his home he impaled his left eye on one of the faucets. After firefighters cut the pipes he was rushed to the hospital with the faucet still stuck in his head. At the hospital it was impossible for Yi Zhao to fit in the scanner, so a plumber was summoned to remove more than a foot (30 cm) of pipe protruding from his eye, but when this did not work, Zhao simply removed the tap himself.

SIXTH SENSE ■ The parents of a three-year-old girl from Middlesbrough, England, are convinced that she has psychic powers. Emilia Rose Taylor had regularly gone into trances as a baby and once she began to speak, she started talking about various people only she could see, including a smelly old man (who it turned out had previously lived at the house) and her father's twin brother, who had died at the age of four.

WRONG DAY ■ A woman from Norfolk, England, discovered in 2008 that she had been celebrating her birthday on the wrong day for more than a century. Lena Thouless, aged 106, had always thought her birthday was November 23, until her daughter discovered that she was actually born on November 22.

PERFECT GAMES ■ In December 2008, brothers Ed and Tom Shircel from Sheboygan, Wisconsin, each bowled perfect 300 games playing for the same team and in the same game.

GHOST STORY ■ A burglar who broke into a house in Malaysia in 2008 told police he was prevented from escaping by a ghost. He claimed that the supernatural figure had held him captive for three days without food and water.

RING RETURNED ■ After losing a gold ring in 1973 when it slipped through a crack in the floorboards of a chapel at Gwyddelwern, Wales, Carys Williams got it back 35 years later when the building was demolished.

TIME RIDDLE ■ Archeologists who opened an ancient Chinese tomb that had been sealed shut more than 400 years ago were alarmed to discover a 100-year-old Swiss watch inside. Believing they were the first people to visit the Ming Dynasty grave in Shangsi since the occupant's death, they were unable to explain the presence of the modern timepiece.

SECRET SISTERS ■ Two women who had been friends for more than 30 years found out in 2008 that they were actually sisters. Deborah Day was adopted at the age of two months, separating her from her sister, Marilyn Morris, but the two met again as teenagers in Weston-super-Mare in Somerset, England, and became firm friends without realizing they were related.

SKULL MYSTERY ■ Scientists on New Zealand's North Island have discovered a skull belonging to a European white woman who lived about 270 years ago—a century before the first-known white settlers arrived in the country.

FATHER FIGURE ■ A one-legged man who has already fathered 78 children is hoping to father 100 by 2015. Born in 1947, Daad Mohammed Murad Abdul Rahman of the United Arab Emirates had already been married 15 times by the age of 60, although he had to divorce his wives as he went along, because under Islamic law he is not allowed to be married to more than four at a time.

BURIED ALIVE ■ Ruby the Border Terrier survived in 2008 despite being buried alive for 16 days in a garden compost heap. She had become trapped under a rock that was meant to stop rabbits from getting into the garden at her home in West Sussex, England.

HAIRY HUMANS ■ There are as many hairs per square inch on your body as on a chimpanzee—but most are too fine or too fair to be visible.

FIRE PROOF ■ Skip and Linda Miller of Cuyamaca, California, have had two houses destroyed by wildfires in four years so have decided to build their third house out of concrete, partially underground and with heat and fire-resistant materials.

VIDEO PUNISHMENT ■ A journalist in Romania can be jailed for up to seven years for recording and showing a video of an official taking a bribe.

UNDERGROUND FIRE ■ An underground fire in coal mines beneath Centralia, Pennsylvania, has been burning since 1962.

NAVAL MYSTERY ■ Although Bolivia has no sea ports and no coastline, it maintains a naval force with more than 150 boats and thousands of sailors.

A Taste for Toothpaste

Dentist Dr. Val Kolpakov from Saginaw, Michigan, collects toothpaste—and since 2002 he has acquired nearly 1,500 different types from around the world. Among his prized possessions are a special Hopalong Cassidy toothpaste and a Scotch whiskey flavored toothpaste.

I Love You

Incredible Eyeful

Ping Zui of Hubei, China, can blow up balloons using only his eyes. Ping, who discovered his talent as a child while swimming in a river, wears a pair of goggles with a plastic pipeline linked to the balloon.

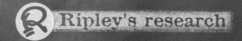

Ripley's research

Ping Zui inflates the balloons through his tear ducts—the only exit for air in the eyes. The tear duct is extremely narrow and winding, and the amount of air that can be expelled in that way is tiny, making his feat all-the-more amazing.

Glandular Fever

This French woman—known as the "Female Gorilla"—suffered from glandular excess, which resulted in huge lumps and masses of dark hair appearing over large parts of her body.

LONG-EARED LADY

Iban women of Sarawak, Malaysia, traditionally wear wooden or metal weights and eardrops around their stretched lobes because elongated ears are a sign of great beauty and status among the tribe.

JACK AND JACKIE ■ Jack and Jackie Reppard from Nokomis, Florida, were born at the same time, in the same room, and were delivered by the same doctor. This may not have proved exceptional in itself, but they went on to attend the same school, graduated together, got married, and have recently celebrated their 40th wedding anniversary!

HEDGEHOG HURLER ■ A man was charged with assaulting a teenage boy in Whakatane, New Zealand, in 2008—with a hedgehog. He picked up the creature and threw it at the boy from a distance of 15 ft (4.5 m), causing a large, red welt and several puncture marks on the victim's body.

PALM ROBBER ■ A man tried to rob a store in DeLand, Florida, in June 2008 with a palm frond as a weapon. He threatened to stab the clerk with the frond if he didn't hand over cash. A customer chased him out of the store with a bar stool.

UP FOR SALE ■ Ian Usher from Perth, Australia, sold his entire life for $380,000 on eBay following the breakdown of his marriage. The sale price included his home, his car, his motorcycle, a two-week trial in his job, and even his friends.

VANISHING POOL ■ Thieves stole a swimming pool containing 1,000 gal (3,785 l) of water from the backyard of a house in Paterson, New Jersey, without spilling a drop. The Valdivia family awoke to find the hip-high, inflatable, 10-ft-diameter (3-m) pool gone, but with no sign of any of the water.

LETTER RETURNED ■ In July 2008, Xan Wedel of Lawrence, Kansas, received a return-to-sender letter that had originally been sent by a previous resident at that address—60 years earlier! The letter, postmarked November 11, 1948, described the town's dismay at Harry S Truman's presidential victory.

GNOME RUSTLER ■ A man was arrested in Brittany, France, in 2008 on suspicion of stealing 170 ornamental gnomes from various people's gardens.

Alas Poor André

A concert pianist whose dying wish was to be part of a stage production of Shakespeare's *Hamlet* has finally realized his ambition. When André Tchaikovsky died in 1982, he left his body to medical research but requested that his skull be given to the Royal Shakespeare Company "for use in theatrical performance." Many actors and directors were uncomfortable with using a real skull but, in 2008, British actor David Tennant held aloft André's skull in *Hamlet* in Stratford-upon-Avon, England.

FIGHTING GRANNY ■ Italian soldiers are prepared for army life by being beaten up on a daily basis by a tiny 77-year-old grandmother. Japanese granny Keiko Wakabayshi may be only 5 ft (1.5 m) tall, but she is a trained master in a variety of martial arts, including judo and karate.

FASHIONABLY LATE ■ Kenneth Smith attended his high school prom in Chester, Pennsylvania, in June 2008—more than 60 years late. The 84-year-old was drafted into military service in 1943 before finishing high school and, although he returned home after World War II, he never received his high school diploma.

HYPNOTIC HEIST ■ An Italian criminal hypnotized supermarket checkout staff into handing over money from their cash registers, leaving them with no memory of the robbery. The last thing they remembered before finding the till empty was the thief leaning over and saying "Look into my eyes."

SAME INITIALS ■ All 11 members of the Lawrence family from Derby, England, have the same initials—T.J. In 2007, Tim James and Teresa Jean called their ninth child Tillie Jasmine—following on from Timothy John, Tara Jessica, Thomas Joseph, twins Taylia Jade and Travis James, Taylor Jake, Thad Jack, and Trey Jacob.

DIRTY LAUNDRY ■ The laundry of a man in Kaiserslautern, Germany, was so foul-smelling that his neighbors called the police, thinking someone had died in the apartment.

REELED IN ■ A man drowning in Maine's Kennebec River in July 2008 was rescued by someone reeling him in with a fishing rod. Bob Greene of Hallowell snagged the man's shirt with a fishing lure and saved him.

Canine Miracle

Marco Menozzi could not believe his eyes when he discovered a dog stuck in the front bumper of his car in Cozze, southern Italy. Traveling at 70 mph (113 km/h), he had struck the animal so hard that it became lodged in the grill. Incredibly, the lucky dog suffered only a broken leg and thankfully is now fully recovered.

Cough Shot

In 1863, W.V. Meadows of West Point, Georgia, was shot in the eye at the Battle of Vicksburg during the American Civil War. He survived, and 58 years later was surprised to cough up the bullet.

Enlarged photo of bullet

Mr. W.V. Meadows
West Point - Ga

CHANCE CANCELLATION ■ Elsa Oliver from Gateshead, England, canceled a vacation to New York just before takeoff because she had a premonition that something really good was going to happen to her. Later that day, she heard she had been selected to appear on the TV quiz show "Who Wants To Be A Millionaire?," and she went on to win £64,000 (over $100,000).

FORESAW DEATH ■ In 1980, U.S. actor David Janssen, star of the TV show *The Fugitive*, had a bad dream in which he saw himself being carried away in a coffin following a heart attack. The dream unnerved him so much that he consulted a psychic, who advised him to have a medical. Two days later, Janssen died from a sudden heart attack.

LUCKY FIND ■ While at summer camp in Connecticut, Brandon Lavallee found 21 four-leaf clovers and two with five leaves—in one day.

TURKEY BOWL ■ Cincinnati, Ohio, prepares for Thanksgiving each year with its traditional Turkey Bowl, where competitors use frozen turkeys instead of bowling balls to play the game.

CLEARED NAME ■ New Jersey lawyer Adam Goodmann took nearly two years and went through five judges to clear himself of a shoplifting conviction. The amount in the dispute was just $3.76 on a special-offer set of photo prints.

Name Dropper

When George Garratt from Somerset, England, wanted to do something different, he officially changed his name to "Captain Fantastic Faster than Superman Spiderman Batman Wolverine The Hulk and the Flash Combined!"

Captain Fantastic Faster than Superman Spiderman Batman Wolverine The Hulk and the FLASH COMBINED!

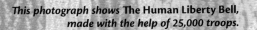

This photograph shows **The Human Liberty Bell,** made with the help of 25,000 troops.

This machine-gun insignia was made with 22,500 officers and men, some lying, some sitting and some standing, at Camp Hancock, Augusta, Georgia, in 1918.

Mole's **Human Statue of Liberty** *was almost eight times the height of the real statue in New York.*

Bird's Eye Art

Arthur Mole was a photographer with an unusually large imagination, taking pictures of tens of thousands of painstakingly organized soldiers on the ground using a regular camera from an 80-ft (24-m) tower.

Viewed from this height, the troops formed vast portraits of patriotic and military symbols. Working as a commercial photographer in Chicago in the early 20th century, Mole saw an opportunity to make inspiring pictures that would encourage support for U.S. troops during World War I.

He would spend at least a week organizing each photograph with his colleague John

Thomas, directing the assembled troops with a megaphone according to a picture drawn on the lens of his camera. Assistants would then trace the outline with extremely long pieces of lace, enabling him to determine precisely how many troops he would require for each photograph.

Arthur Mole's most famous creations were captured in 1918. Twenty-five thousand soldiers from Camp Dix, New Jersey, stood as one to create *The Human Liberty Bell*, and 18,000 men assembled to Mole's orders in a vast rendering of the Statue of Liberty that stretched for 1,200 ft (365 m). Possibly his most dramatic image involved 21,000 men at Camp Sherman, Ohio, to make *The Living Portrait of Woodrow Wilson*—the U.S. president at the time.

Mole's largest work saw 30,000 men carefully placed to create this **Human U.S. Shield** *at Camp Custer in Battle Creek, Michigan.*

Mole's incredible portrait of President Woodrow Wilson.

Sincerely Yours,

Woodrow Wilson

,000 OFFICERS AND MEN
MP SHERMAN, CHILLICOTHE OHIO
G. GEN. MATHEW C. SMITH, COMMANDING

LIVING PHOTOGRAPHY

> The Mayhart Studio of Chicago enlisted the services of hundreds of people to form *A Living Flag*—the Stars and Stripes—in 1917.

> In 1947, Eugene Omar Goldbeck of San Antonio, Texas, arranged 21,765 men at his local air base to represent the American Air Force insignia.

> Advertising agency executive Paul Arden created the 1989 British Airways TV commercial in which thousands of people from all over the world converged on Utah to form a smiling face.

> New Yorker Spencer Tunick has been photographing masses of naked people in public locations since 1992. In 2007, he posed 18,000 nude people in Mexico City—all crouched in the fetal position.

ACKNOWLEDGMENTS

COVER (l) toothpasteworld.com, (b/r) Canadian Press/Rex Features; BACK COVER Discovery Channel "Wild Child"/Discovery Communications; 4 toothpasteworld.com; 6–7 Barcroft Media Ltd/Scrabble, the distinctive game board and letter tiles, and all associated logos are trademarks of Hasbro in the United States and Canada and are used with permission. © 2009 Hasbro. All Rights Reserved. Scrabble ® is a registered trademark of J. W. Spears & Sons Ltd., a subsidiary of Mattel, Inc. © Mattel, Inc. All Rights Reserved.; 8 (t) swns.com, (b) Yawar Nazir/Scoopt/Getty Images; 9 Mark Ralston/AFP/Getty Images; 10 (t) © EuroPics[CEN], (b) Discovery Channel "Wild Child"/Discovery Communications; 11 Canadian Press/Rex Features; 12–13 AP Photo/Kyodo News; 14 Barcroft Media; 15 Reuters/David Moir; 16 (t, l) Blank Archives/Getty Images, (r) Hulton Archive/Getty Images; 17 (r) Hulton Archive/Getty Images; 21 (b) Blank Archives/Getty Images; 23 Henry Guttmann/Getty Images; 24 (b) www.theyrecoming.com; 25 (t) Reuters/Ho New, (b) Tim Sloan/AFP/Getty Images; 26 Reuters//Sukree Sukplang; 27 (t) © EuroPics[CEN], (b) toothpasteworld.com; 28 (l) ChinaFotoPress/Photocome/PA Photos; 28–29 © Bettmann/Corbis; 29 (r) © Karen Kasmauski/Corbis; 30 (t) Bournemouth News/Rex Features, (b) © EuroPics[CEN]; 31 (b) swns.com; 32–33 Library of Congress

Key: t = top, b = bottom, c = center, l = left, r = right, sp = single page, dp = double page

All other photos are from Ripley Entertainment Inc.
Every attempt has been made to acknowledge correctly and contact copyright holders and we apologize in advance for any unintentional errors or omissions, which will be corrected in future editions.